#2⁰⁰

On the Side

GENERAL EDITOR
CHUCK WILLIAMS

RECIPES
JOYCE GOLDSTEIN AND OTHER CONTRIBUTORS

PHOTOGRAPHY
ALLAN ROSENBERG AND ALLEN V. LOTT

TIME
LIFE
BOOKS

TIME-LIFE BOOKS
Time-Life Books is a division of Time Life Inc.
Time-Life is a trademark of Time-Warner Inc. U.S.A.

Time-Life Custom Publishing
Vice President and Publisher: Terry Newell
Managing Editor: Donia Ann Steele
Director of Acquisitions: Jennifer L. Pearce
Vice President of Sales and Marketing: Neil Levin
Director of Financial Operations: J. Brian Birky

WILLIAMS-SONOMA
Founder and Vice Chairman: Chuck Williams
Book Buyer: Victoria Kalish

WELDON OWEN INC.
President: John Owen
Vice President and Publisher: Wendely Harvey
Chief Operating Officer: Larry Partington
Vice President International Sales: Stuart Laurence
Managing Editor: Judith Dunham
Consulting Editor: Norman Kolpas
Copy Editor: Sharon Silva
Design: John Bull, The Book Design Company
Production Director: Stephanie Sherman
Production Manager: Jen Dalton
Production Consultant: Sarah Lemas
Production Editor: Deborah Cowder
Food Photographers: Allan Rosenberg, Allen V. Lott
Additional Food Photography: Chris Shorten
Food Stylists: Heidi Gintner, Susan Massey,
    John Phillip Carroll, Peggy Fallon
Prop Stylists: Sandra Griswold, Karen Nicks
Glossary Illustrations: Alice Harth

The Williams-Sonoma Kitchen Library
conceived and produced by Weldon Owen Inc.
814 Montgomery St., San Francisco, CA 94133

In collaboration with Williams-Sonoma
3250 Van Ness Ave., San Francisco, CA 94109

Printed in China by Toppan Printing Co., (HK) Ltd.

A Note on Weights and Measures:
All recipes include customary U.S. and metric
measurements. Metric conversions are based on
a standard developed for these books and have
been rounded off. Actual weights may vary.

A Weldon Owen Production

Copyright © 1998 Weldon Owen Inc.
Reprinted in 1998

Library of Congress
Cataloging-in-Publication Data:

Goldstein, Joyce Esersky.
    On the side / [recipes, Joyce Goldstein] ; general editor, Chuck
Williams . photography, Allan Rosenberg and Allen V. Lott.
        p.   cm. — (Williams-Sonoma kitchen library)
    Includes index.
    ISBN 0-7370-2001-6
    1. Side dishes (Cookery) 2. Cookery (Vegetables) I. Williams,
Chuck.   II. Title.   III. Series.
TX801.G615   1998
641.8'1—dc21   98-9542
                                                                        CIP

Contents

INTRODUCTION

So often in life, we hear someone remark that "it's the little things that make all the difference." This universal truth certainly extends to the world of food.

How many times have you come away from a good meal singing the praises not of the appetizer, main course, or dessert but of some remarkable dish that was served on the side? Maybe it was a fresh seasonal vegetable, quickly cooked and seasoned in an innovative way. Perhaps it was an unusual dressing or condiment that sparked up a holiday roast. Or a rice dish that nicely soaked up the savory sauce of a stew or sauté. Or a fresh, crisp salad that made the perfect complement to a main course hot off the outdoor grill.

This book is dedicated to just such side dishes. It begins with step-by-step guides to the basic preparation of ingredients. Following those fundamentals are 45 recipes, divided into separate sections on salads, vegetables, potatoes and dressings, beans and grains, and condiments. A comprehensive, illustrated glossary of featured side dish ingredients concludes the book.

I hope that, once you've familiarized yourself with its comprehensive and varied contents, you'll refer to this book again and again as a source of quick, easy side dishes. Simple though they might be, they have the power to elevate any meal far beyond the ordinary.

Chuck Williams

SIDE DISH BASICS

Given the nature of the role they play in a menu and the ingredients they feature, side dishes should be simple to prepare. After all, it doesn't make sense to expend more effort on an accompaniment than on the main course. Fortunately, most ingredients used in side dishes require minimal effort to ready them for cooking.

Nevertheless, you will want to observe some essential techniques and preparation steps, demonstrated here and on the following pages. They range from cleaning and trimming fresh produce (right) and peeling away skins from tomatoes and pearl onions (opposite) to readying dried beans for cooking (page 8), puréeing potatoes (page 9), cooking the Italian-style cornmeal mush known as polenta (page 11), and preparing two versatile stocks, vegetable and chicken (pages 12–13), used in many recipes in this book.

On an even more basic level, it makes good sense to shop carefully for the best-quality ingredients. When choosing recipes, consider not only your overall menu, but also which produce is in season. Opt for fresh vegetables and fruits with a good, bright color, free from blemishes. Any leaves should look bright and crisp, without signs of drying or wilting. Quality produce will generally feel heavy for its size, an indication that it has not dried out.

When selecting dried beans and grains, seek out sources that have a regular turnover of stock, which will lessen the chance of buying older, drier products that will take longer to cook. Avoid any specimens that lack uniformity or otherwise look unusual in size, shape, or color, or that show any signs of mold from improper drying. Buy only as much as you are likely to use within a few months.

CLEANING VEGETABLES

Mushrooms, spinach, and leeks, because of the conditions in which they are grown, contain grit, dirt, or sand that must be removed before the vegetables are used. If desired, cut off the stems from the mushrooms before cleaning. To facilitate rinsing spinach, snip off the tough stems from the leaves. After following the special cleaning techniques below, prepare the vegetables as directed in individual recipes.

Brushing mushrooms.
A specially made brush like the one shown here can be used to gently dislodge and sweep away any dirt or grit from the surface of each mushroom. Avoid rinsing mushrooms in water, which will make them soggy.

Rinsing spinach.
Place the spinach leaves in a large bowl filled with cold water. Agitate the leaves in the water, then lift out the spinach and discard the dirty water. Repeat the process until the rinsing water is clear when the leaves are removed.

Rinsing leeks.
Remove the root end and cut off the tough green portion of the leaves. Cut each leek lengthwise to reveal the inner layers. Vigorously swish each leek in a bowl of cold water, separating the layers to wash away any grit trapped inside.

PEELING & SEEDING TOMATOES

When tomatoes are made into sauces—as for Polenta with Tomato Sauce (page 85)—or are combined with other ingredients, their skins and/or seeds are removed to enhance the taste and texture of the final dish.

1. Cutting an X in the skins.
Bring a saucepan three-fourths full of water to a boil. Using a small, sharp knife, cut a shallow X in the skin at the base of each tomato. Cut out the core from the stem end of the tomato.

2. Boiling the tomatoes.
Submerge the tomatoes in the boiling water for 20–30 seconds to loosen the skins. Using a slotted spoon, remove from the water and immerse in a bowl of cold water.

3. Peeling the tomatoes and removing the seeds.
Using the sharp knife—or your fingertips—and starting at the X, peel the skin from each tomato. Cut the tomato in half lengthwise. Holding the tomato over a bowl, squeeze it gently to force out the seed sacs.

PEELING PEARL ONIONS

Bite-sized pearl onions can be eaten whole. Before they are cooked, they are trimmed and peeled so they retain their shape.

1. Boiling the onions.
Bring a saucepan three-fourths full of water to a boil. Evenly trim off the root end of each onion and cut a shallow X in the trimmed end. Immerse the onions in the boiling water for about 2 minutes.

2. Removing the skins.
Drain the onions and submerge in cold water. Gently squeeze each onion with your fingertips to slip off the skin. Discard the skins and use the onions whole as directed in the recipe.

Sorting, Soaking & Cooking Beans

Whether you buy dried beans prepackaged or in bulk, they are likely to include a few small stones or fibers that must be removed before cooking; this step also lets you eliminate any discolored or misshapen specimens. After the beans are picked over, a thorough rinsing in a colander or sieve with cold running water will wash away any dust clinging to their surfaces.

Once the beans are clean, they should be presoaked to rehydrate them, thus ensuring even, thorough cooking. Older recipes usually call for 8 to 12 hours of presoaking, which is no longer necessary thanks to modern methods of drying beans. Today, most beans need to soak for only about 3 hours. The beans, combined with plenty of cold water, can be set aside at room temperature. As soon as soaking has been completed, the beans are ready for cooking.

To make the process go even faster, the beans can be quick-soaked. Place the beans in a saucepan with water to cover by at least 2 inches (5 cm). Bring to a simmer, then remove from the heat. Cover the pot and let the beans stand for 1–1½ hours before draining them and continuing with the recipe.

When the beans are cooked, an additional step may be followed, if desired. After slowly being brought to a full boil, the beans are boiled for a full 10 minutes; the high temperature helps to neutralize natural toxins in the beans, which would otherwise cause gastric distress. Once this boiling period is over, the temperature is then reduced to a simmer and the beans continue cooking until tender.

1. Picking over the beans.
Carefully sort through the beans and remove any impurities such as stones, fibers, or discolored or misshapen specimens. Place the beans in a colander and rinse thoroughly.

2. Soaking the beans.
Place the rinsed beans in a bowl, cover with plenty of cold water, and let soak for 3 hours. The beans will absorb some of the water.

Chickpeas (Garbanzo Beans)

Red Kidney Beans

Flageolets

Small White (Navy) Beans

SELECTING & PURÉEING POTATOES

Home cooks today have a wide range of choices when shopping for potatoes. Those labeled "baking," "russet," or "Idaho" are large and have thick brown skins; their floury, dry texture makes them ideal for baking, mashing, or deep-frying. Medium-sized "white" potatoes have thin, tan skins and, when cooked, a texture finer than baking potatoes but coarser than waxy yellow varieties, making them a good all-purpose choice.

Thin-skinned "yellow" potatoes have yellow-tinged waxy flesh, suitable for steaming, boiling, sautéing, or roasting; look for such special varieties as Yellow Finn and Yukon gold potatoes, prized for their buttery taste. "Red" potatoes have thin, red skins and waxy white flesh, and are good steamed, boiled, or roasted. Potatoes labeled "new" are any variety harvested while still immature, when the flesh is tender and sweet and the skins are fragile.

Sweet potatoes are tubers enjoyed for the sweet flavor of their pale yellow to orange flesh. Most common is the light-skinned variety. Less common yam types, not actually true Caribbean yams, have darker skins and very sweet, deep orange flesh.

When buying any variety of potatoes, look for firm, well-formed specimens free from blemishes, bruises, or sprouting eyes. Avoid any with green spots, caused by a toxic alkaloid resulting from exposure to light. Do not wash potatoes before storing, which can cause spoilage. Store the potatoes, unbagged or loosely wrapped in brown paper, in a dark place at cool room temperature.

When puréeing potatoes, use a food mill or ricer, or mash them by hand with a sturdy potato masher. A food processor will yield gummy results.

Using a food mill.
Fit a food mill with the fine or coarse puréeing disk, depending on the texture desired, and place over a bowl. Put the cooked potatoes into the mill and turn the handle to force the potatoes through the disk.

Using a ricer.
A ricer yields smooth, creamy mashed potatoes. Working over a bowl, put the cooked potatoes in the ricer and press down on the handle to force them through the tiny holes.

New Potatoes

Yellow Potatoes

Yam-Type Sweet Potatoes

Baking Potatoes

Red Potatoes

White Potatoes

Sweet Potatoes

9

SEEDING & ROASTING BELL PEPPERS

The flavorless and indigestible seeds and ribs of bell peppers (capsicums) should be removed before the peppers are used in a recipe. The peppers can then be roasted, a technique that brings out the sweet flavor and tender texture of their flesh.

4. Peeling the skins.
Uncover the peppers and peel away the blackened skins, using your fingertips or a small knife. Then cut or tear the peppers as directed in the recipe.

1. Halving the peppers.
Cut each bell pepper in half lengthwise through the stem end to expose the inner ribs and cluster of seeds.

2. Removing the stems, seeds, and ribs.
Pull out the stem section, along with the attached cluster of seeds. Remove the white ribs, or membranes, and any remaining seeds. Preheat a broiler (griller) and place the pepper halves, cut sides down, on a baking sheet.

3. Roasting the peppers.
Broil the peppers about 4 inches (10 cm) below the heat source until the skins evenly blacken and blister. Remove from the broiler, then drape the peppers loosely with aluminum foil and let steam and cool for about 10 minutes.

COOKING ASPARAGUS SPEARS

To ensure the best result, purchase spears of uniform thickness. Remove the tough ends and, if necessary, peel the fibrous outer layer from the spears before cooking. Choose a large, wide pan that will accommodate all the asparagus without crowding and allow the spears to cook evenly.

1. Trimming and peeling the spears.
Snap off any woody ends. Use a vegetable peeler to remove the thin skin from any thick stalks, starting 2 inches (5 cm) below the tip. Bring a frying pan half filled with salted water to a boil.

2. Boiling the spears.
Add the asparagus to the boiling water and cook until tender-crisp when pierced, 4–6 minutes; the timing will depend on the thickness of the stalks. Immerse in cold water, drain well, and pat dry.

GRATING AND CUTTING CITRUS ZEST

The thin, outermost layer of a lemon, lime, or other citrus fruit contains most of the fruit's aromatic essential oils. When zest is grated or cut into strips, it is used to add its distinctive freshness to flavored butters (page 29), tomato sauce (page 44), and conserves (page 98).

Grating zest with a hand-held grater.
Lightly rub the fruit against the small rasps of a handheld grater. Be careful to remove the colored zest only and not the bitter white pith underneath it.

Using a zester.
A simple specialized tool called a zester has sharp-edged holes that remove the zest in thin shreds. To use a zester, draw the holes across the skin of the fruit.

Cutting zest strips.
Holding the edge of a paring knife almost parallel to the skin of the fruit, cut off the zest in wide strips, again taking care not to remove the white pith. Alternatively, use a vegetable peeler in place of the knife.

PREPARING POLENTA

Follow the steps below to ensure a smooth, creamy result when making polenta for side dishes.

1. Adding the polenta to water.
To simmering water, add the polenta in a thin, steady stream, stirring constantly with a wooden spoon to prevent the grains from clumping.

2. Cooking the polenta.
As the polenta cooks, stir it constantly with the wooden spoon until it is thick and creamy and begins to pull away from the sides of the pan. Remove from the heat and use as directed in individual recipes.

WORKING WITH CHEESE

Grating hard cheeses.
Draw the cheese across a half-cylindrical grater, shown here, or box grater.

Shaving cheese.
Draw a vegetable peeler, shown here, or cheese shaver across the block of cheese.

Making Vegetable Stock

All stocks, whether made from vegetables, shown here, or from poultry (opposite), meat, or seafood, rely on slow simmering to extract the essence of the featured ingredients into the water. After the vegetable stock has cooled, it can be stored in the refrigerator for up to 4 days or in the freezer for up to 3 months.

1. Roasting the vegetables. After coating a roasting pan with nonstick spray, evenly arrange the vegetables in the pan. Roast until well browned on all sides. Stir during roasting with a spatula or spoon to ensure even cooking.

2. Skimming the stock. After the vegetables, water, and seasonings come to a boil, impurities rise to the surface in the form of froth or scum. Use a ladle or large metal spoon to skim them off and discard.

3. Straining the stock. Ladle the stock and vegetables into a colander or sieve set over a bowl. Discard the solids and refrigerate the stock until cool, then store as directed.

Vegetable Stock

This flavorful stock is made by roasting the vegetables before they are simmered. If you like, use it in recipes that call for chicken stock as well as in those made with vegetable stock.

7 large carrots, unpeeled, cut into chunks
3 yellow onions, unpeeled, quartered
8 celery stalks, cut into chunks
½ lb (250 g) fresh mushrooms with stems intact, brushed clean and quartered
1 large baking potato, unpeeled, cut into chunks
2 cups (16 fl oz/500 ml) plus 4½ qt (4.5 l) water
4–6 fresh thyme or parsley sprigs, or a mixture
¼ teaspoon whole peppercorns, crushed
1 bay leaf

Preheat an oven to 350°F (180°C). Coat a large roasting pan with nonstick cooking spray.

Spread the carrots, onions, celery, mushrooms, and potato in the pan. Roast, stirring once or twice, for 45 minutes to 1 hour, or for up to 1½ hours if you want a more strongly flavored stock.

Remove the pan from the oven and transfer the vegetables to a large stockpot. Add the 2 cups (16 fl oz/ 500 ml) water to the roasting pan, then stir and scrape the bottom with a spatula to dislodge any browned bits. Add the liquid to the stockpot along with the 4½ qt (4.5 l) water, thyme and/or parsley, peppercorns, and bay leaf. Bring to a boil over high heat, skimming off any scum or froth that rises to the surface. Reduce the heat to low, cover partially, and simmer for 2 hours.

Strain the stock through a colander or sieve into a large bowl. Discard the solids and place the stock in the refrigerator to cool completely.

Makes about 4 qt (4 l)

Carrot and Blue Cheese Salad with Cumin

2 oz (60 g) blue cheese, at room temperature
1 cup (8 fl oz/250 ml) light (single) cream
salt to taste
2 tablespoons Asian sesame oil
1 lb (500 g) carrots, peeled and thinly sliced
1 tablespoon cumin seeds

At once rich, tangy, sweet, and spicy, this tasty salad goes best with simple dishes such as grilled meats or omelets. Celery makes an interesting substitute for all or part of the carrots. Sesame, poppy, or mustard seeds can replace the cumin seeds.

✦

In a blender or a food processor, combine the cheese, cream, and salt. Process until mixed. With the motor running, add the oil in a thin, steady stream and continue to blend until the mixture forms a creamy dressing.

Arrange the carrots in a bowl, pour the dressing over the top, sprinkle with the cumin seeds, and serve.

Serves 4

Grilled Corn on the Cob with Chili-Lime Butter

6 ears of corn
6 tablespoons (3 oz/90 g) unsalted butter,
  at room temperature
1 tablespoon chili powder
½ teaspoon paprika
¼ teaspoon cayenne pepper
grated zest of 1 lime
2 tablespoons lime juice

A hint of citrus and chili powder highlights the natural sweetness of the corn, making this side dish a show-stopper for any summertime backyard or picnic barbecue. Serve with extra lime wedges to squeeze over the corn.

❖

Prepare a fire in a charcoal grill.

Remove the husks and silks from the corn. In a bowl, mix together the butter, chili powder, paprika, cayenne, lime zest, and lime juice. Spread 1 tablespoon of the chile-lime butter on each ear of corn, then wrap each ear in a large piece of aluminum foil.

When the coals are hot, arrange the corn on the grill rack 4–6 inches (10–15 cm) above the coals. Grill, turning once or twice with tongs, for 10 minutes.

Remove and discard the foil and serve the corn immediately.

Serves 6

Baked Ratatouille

1 large eggplant (aubergine)

2 zucchini (courgettes)

2 red or green bell peppers (capsicums), or one of each

½ lb (250 g) fresh mushrooms, brushed clean

1 yellow onion

⅓ cup (3 oz/90 g) tomato paste

⅓ cup (3 fl oz/80 ml) red or white wine vinegar

¼ cup (2 fl oz/60 ml) water

2 tablespoons olive oil

2 cloves garlic, minced

1 tablespoon chopped fresh thyme or 1 teaspoon dried

1 teaspoon salt

½ teaspoon ground pepper

½ cup (¾ oz/20 g) chopped fresh basil or parsley

The communal baking of the vegetables blends their flavors deliciously. Serve ratatouille hot or cold with meat or poultry. It will keep for up to 4 days in the refrigerator.

❖❖

Preheat an oven to 400° F (200° C). Coat a large roasting pan with nonstick cooking spray. As you prepare each of the following vegetables, add it to the prepared pan: Cut the unpeeled eggplant into 1-inch (2.5-cm) cubes. Cut the zucchini crosswise into rounds ½ inch (12 mm) thick. Halve the bell peppers through their stem ends and remove the stems, ribs, and seeds. Cut the peppers into 1-inch (2.5-cm) squares. Depending upon the size of the mushrooms, cut them into halves or quarters. Thinly slice the onion.

In a small bowl, combine the tomato paste, vinegar, water, olive oil, garlic, thyme, salt, and pepper and stir until blended and smooth. Add to the roasting pan, then stir and toss to combine and coat the vegetables evenly.

Bake until the vegetables begin to soften, about 30 minutes, stirring once at the halfway point. Reduce the heat to 325°F (165°C). Cover the roasting pan and bake until the vegetables are soft and tender but not mushy, about 30 minutes longer, stirring every 10 minutes.

Remove from the oven, uncover the ratatouille and let stand for 10 minutes. Stir in the basil or parsley and serve hot, at room temperature, or cold.

Serves 6

Brussels Sprouts with Garlic and Parmesan

1½ lb (750 g) brussels sprouts
2 tablespoons unsalted butter
2 tablespoons olive oil
6 large cloves garlic, minced
¾–1 cup (6–8 fl oz/180–250 ml)
  Chicken Stock (*recipe on page 13*)
  or broth
salt and ground pepper to taste
¾ cup (3 oz/90 g) grated Parmesan
  cheese

The sprouts stand up well to the large quantity of garlic in this vivid green, quickly cooked dish.

❖❖

Trim the ends from the brussels sprouts and cut the sprouts in half lengthwise. Select a sauté pan large enough to hold all the sprouts in a single layer and place over low heat. Add the butter and olive oil and, when the butter melts, add the garlic. Sauté until softened, about 2 minutes.

Add the brussels sprouts and the stock or broth to a depth of 1½ inches (4 cm), cover, and simmer, stirring occasionally, until crisp, 5–8 minutes. Season with salt and pepper.

Transfer to a warmed serving bowl and sprinkle the cheese over the top. Serve at once.

Serves 6

Stuffed Eggplant

3 baby globe eggplants (aubergines) or
  6 Asian (slender) eggplants
salt, as needed
½ cup (4 fl oz/125 ml) plus
  2 tablespoons olive oil
1 large yellow onion, chopped
4 large cloves garlic, minced
1 tablespoon dried oregano
1½ cups (9 oz/280 g) peeled and diced
  tomatoes
¼ cup (⅓ oz/10 g) chopped fresh parsley
ground pepper to taste
½ cup (4 fl oz/125 ml) water

The eggplant shells are precooked to make them tender and completely edible. Serve the stuffed shells with a main-course roast.

⚬⚬⚬

Cut the eggplants in half lengthwise. Using a sharp knife, score the flesh and remove most of the pulp from each half, leaving shells ¼ inch (6 mm) thick. Dice the pulp and set aside. Salt the eggplant shells and place, cut sides down, in a colander. Let stand for 1 hour. Rinse and pat dry.

Preheat an oven to 350°F (180°C). Oil a baking dish large enough to hold the eggplant halves in a single layer.

Warm 2 tablespoons of the olive oil in a large sauté pan. Add the onion and sauté until translucent and tender, about 10 minutes. Transfer to a bowl. In the same pan, heat 6 tablespoons (3 fl oz/90 ml) of the olive oil, add the diced eggplant, and cook, stirring often, until softened, about 5 minutes. Stir in the garlic, oregano, and tomatoes and cook until the eggplant is tender, about 3 minutes. Transfer the eggplant mixture to the bowl with the onion. Add the parsley and mix well. Season with salt and pepper.

In a large sauté pan over low heat, warm the remaining 2 tablespoons oil. Working in batches if necessary, add the eggplant shells and cook, turning once or twice, for a few minutes to soften them. Transfer to the prepared baking dish, placing them hollow sides up and side by side. Stuff with the eggplant mixture, dividing evenly. Add the water to the dish, cover, and bake until very tender, about 45 minutes.

Transfer to a warmed serving platter or individual plates and serve immediately.

Serves 6

Corn with Chiles and Coconut Milk

2 pasilla chiles
1 teaspoon cumin seeds
2 tablespoons unsalted butter
¼ cup (¾ oz/20 g) minced green (spring) onions, including tender green tops
1 tablespoon ground coriander
1 teaspoon curry powder
⅛ teaspoon cayenne pepper
1 cup (8 fl oz/250 ml) coconut milk
½ cup (4 fl oz/125 ml) Chicken Stock (*recipe on page 13*) or broth
1 teaspoon grated lemon zest
4 cups (1½ lb/750 g) corn kernels (6–8 ears)
¼ cup (⅓ oz/10 g) chopped fresh cilantro (fresh coriander)
salt and ground black pepper to taste

Incredibly sweet and aromatic, curried corn is a wonderful companion to spicy chicken or meat courses. Summer white corn is best, but during the winter you may use frozen corn as well. The dish can be prepared up to the point when the coconut milk, stock, and lemon zest are added 2 hours in advance and then finished just before serving.

❧

Preheat a broiler (griller). Place the chiles on a baking sheet and slip under the broiler. Broil (grill), turning as needed, until the skins blacken and blister. Remove from the broiler, drape the chiles loosely with aluminum foil, and let cool for 10 minutes. Using your fingers, peel away the skins. Cut each chile in half and pull out and discard the stems, seeds, and ribs. Chop and set aside.

In a small, dry frying pan over medium heat, toast the cumin seeds, stirring or shaking the pan, until fragrant, about 3 minutes. Transfer to a spice grinder or a mortar and finely grind; set aside.

In a large saucepan over medium heat, melt the butter. Add the green onions and sauté, stirring, until tender, about 5 minutes. Stir in the cumin, coriander, curry powder, and cayenne and sauté for 3 minutes longer to blend the flavors.

Add the coconut milk, stock or broth, and lemon zest and bring to a simmer, stirring to mix well. Add the corn kernels and continue to simmer until the kernels are almost tender, about 3 minutes.

Fold in the reserved chiles and the cilantro and cook for 1 minute longer to heat through. Season to taste with salt and black pepper.

Transfer to a warmed serving dish and serve at once.

Serves 6

Asparagus with Capers and Pine Nuts

¼ cup (1½ oz/45 g) pine nuts
1½ lb (750 g) asparagus, preferably small to medium-sized spears, 6–7 inches (15–18 cm) long
6 tablespoons (3 oz/90 g) unsalted butter
1 tablespoon lemon juice
¼ cup (2 oz/60 g) capers
ground pepper and salt to taste
¼ lb (125g) Parmesan cheese

Serve this dish immediately after cooking, when the heat of the vegetable combines with the other ingredients to produce a lovely fragrance that complements grilled seafood. Small to medium-sized asparagus spears will have the finest flavor and texture. If the capers are very salty, rinse well with cold water and drain before using.

❖❖

*I*n a heavy, dry frying pan over medium heat, toast the pine nuts, stirring, until lightly colored and fragrant, 1–2 minutes. Transfer to a bowl; set aside.

Remove the tough ends of the asparagus spears; trim the spears to a uniform length. If the stalks are thick, using a vegetable peeler or paring knife and starting about 2 inches (5 cm) below the tip, peel off the outer skin.

Half fill a large, wide frying pan with salted water and bring to a boil. Add the asparagus spears and boil until tender-crisp, 4–6 minutes; the timing will depend upon the thickness of the stalks.

Meanwhile, in a small saucepan over medium-low heat, melt the butter. Add the lemon juice and capers, season with pepper, and cook, stirring gently, for 30–40 seconds. Taste and adjust the seasonings with salt, pepper, or lemon juice.

When the asparagus spears are done, drain well and place on a serving platter or individual plates. Spoon the caper sauce over them and then scatter on the pine nuts. Using a vegetable peeler and holding the piece of Parmesan over the asparagus, shave off paper-thin slices; be generous with the cheese. Serve at once.

Serves 6

Honey-Baked Tomatoes with Crusty Topping

1½ cups (3 oz/90 g) fresh bread crumbs
½ cup (4 fl oz/125 ml) olive oil
1 teaspoon salt
½ teaspoon ground pepper
6 tablespoons (4 oz/125 g) honey
pinch of ground nutmeg
6 ripe tomatoes

Old-fashioned and homey, this side dish rounds out down-to-earth main courses from meat loaf to roast chicken. The honey heightens the flavor of even out-of-season tomatoes, although vine-ripened ones are the best choice. If desired, serve each tomato on a plate with a handful of fresh watercress or arugula sprigs for a refreshingly bitter contrast.

❖❖❖

Preheat an oven to 350°F (180°C). Spread the bread crumbs on a baking sheet, toss with 6 tablespoons (3 fl oz/90 ml) of the oil, and sprinkle with ½ teaspoon of the salt and the pepper. Bake, stirring often, until golden and slightly crunchy but not hard, about 20 minutes. Set aside. Leave the oven set at 350°F (180°C).

In a small saucepan over low heat, combine the honey, the remaining 2 tablespoons oil, and the nutmeg and heat, stirring a few times, until warm and thinned to a brushing consistency.

Cut a slice off the stem end of each tomato. Place the tomatoes in a baking dish, stem ends up, and sprinkle evenly with the remaining ½ teaspoon salt. Brush the cut surface of each tomato with a little of the honey mixture and then top each tomato with an equal amount of the bread crumbs, pressing them into the tomato.

Bake, basting with the remaining honey mixture several times, until the tomatoes are soft and lightly browned on top, 15–20 minutes.

Serves 6

Green Beans with Celery and Toasted Almonds

1½–2 lb (750 g–1 kg) green beans, trimmed

¼ cup (2 oz/60 g) unsalted butter or ¼ cup (2 fl oz/60 ml) olive oil

1 cup (3½ oz/105 g) sliced yellow onion

4 large celery stalks, cut on the diagonal into strips ¼ inch (6 mm) wide

1 cup (4 oz/125 g) sliced (flaked) toasted almonds (*see glossary, page 106*) (optional)

salt and ground pepper to taste

You can boil the green beans and toast the nuts up to 4 hours in advance. The dish will then go together quickly at dinnertime, ready to serve alongside roast poultry or meat.

❖❖❖

Bring a large saucepan three-fourths full of salted water to a boil. Add the green beans and boil until tender-crisp, 3–5 minutes. Drain, immerse in ice water to stop the cooking, and drain again. Pat dry with paper towels and cut into 2-inch (5-cm) lengths. Set aside.

In a large sauté pan over medium heat, melt the butter or warm the oil. Add the onion and sauté, stirring, until tender and translucent, 8–10 minutes. Add the celery, raise the heat slightly, and stir and toss until almost tender, 3–4 minutes. Add the green beans and almonds (if using) and heat to serving temperature. Season with salt and pepper.

Transfer to a warmed dish and serve immediately.

Serves 6

Grilled Eggplant with Sweet Cherry Tomato Sauce

¼ cup (2 fl oz/60 ml) olive oil, warmed
1 clove garlic, crushed

For the cherry tomato sauce:
2 cups (12 oz/375 g) stemmed cherry
  tomatoes
½ cup (3½ oz/105 g) firmly packed light
  brown sugar
grated zest of 1 lemon
¼ cup (2 fl oz/60 ml) lemon juice
1 tablespoon peeled and grated fresh
  ginger
3 tablespoons water
½ teaspoon ground cinnamon
½ teaspoon ground cumin
pinch of cayenne pepper
salt and ground black pepper to taste

2 firm globe eggplants (aubergines),
  about ½–¾ lb (250–375 g) each, or
  6 Asian (slender) eggplants
salt and freshly ground black pepper to
  taste

The thick, sweet, and spicy sauce, which resembles a conserve, lends a spicy sweetness to the eggplant. Serve with grilled meats such as lamb or with grilled poultry.

❖

Pour the warmed oil into a small bowl and add the garlic clove. Let stand for 1 hour.

To make the sauce, in a saucepan over medium heat, combine the tomatoes, brown sugar, lemon zest and juice, ginger, water, cinnamon, cumin, and cayenne. Cook uncovered, stirring occasionally, until the tomatoes break down and the mixture becomes thick and syrupy, about 30 minutes. Season with salt and black pepper and remove from the heat. You should have about 1 cup (8 fl oz/250 ml) sauce. At this point, the sauce can be transferred to a jar, covered tightly, and refrigerated for up to 1 week.

While the sauce is cooking, prepare a fire in a charcoal grill. Oil the grill rack and position it 4–6 inches (10–15 cm) above the fire. Alternatively, preheat a broiler (griller).

If using globe eggplants, peel and cut crosswise into slices about 1 inch (2.5 cm) thick. If using Asian eggplants, do not peel; cut each in half lengthwise and score the skin side with the point of a knife. Brush the eggplants with the garlic oil and sprinkle with salt and pepper. Grill or broil the eggplants, turning once, until soft but not too browned, about 3 minutes on each side.

Meanwhile, rewarm the tomato sauce over low heat. When the eggplants are done, divide the slices among 6 plates or place 2 Asian eggplant halves on each. Top with the tomato sauce.

Serves 6

Glazed Carrots with Marsala and Hazelnuts

1 lb (500 g) carrots

1 cup (8 fl oz/250 ml) water

½ teaspoon salt

3 tablespoons unsalted butter

2 shallots, minced

½ cup (4 fl oz/125 ml) dry Marsala, preferably Italian

⅓ cup (3 oz/90 g) sugar

½ cup (2½ oz/75 g) hazelnuts (filberts), toasted and coarsely chopped (see glossary, page 106)

bouquets of fresh aromatic herbs such as mint, rosemary, basil, oregano, and dill, preferably with blossoms

Rich, crunchy hazelnuts seem to add just the right finishing touch to this easy but memorable side dish for meat or poultry.

❖

Peel the carrots and cut in half crosswise. Cut the upper (thicker) portions in half lengthwise so that all the pieces are more or less uniform. In a sauté pan over medium-high heat, combine the carrots, water, salt, and 1 tablespoon of the butter. Bring to a boil, reduce the heat to low, cover tightly, and barely simmer until the carrots are tender when pierced, 10–15 minutes. If the liquid begins to cook away, add a few tablespoons water. Drain, transfer to a plate, and set aside.

In the same pan over medium-low heat, melt the remaining 2 tablespoons butter. Add the shallots and sauté gently, stirring, until translucent, 4–5 minutes. Add the Marsala and sugar and simmer, stirring, until the sugar dissolves. Continue to simmer, stirring occasionally, until thickened to a medium syrup consistency, 4–5 minutes. Return the carrots to the pan, add the chopped hazelnuts, and carefully turn the carrots in the syrup until well coated.

Transfer the carrots to a warmed serving dish or individual plates. Spoon the glaze and hazelnuts over the carrots. Garnish with the herb bouquets and serve immediately.

Serves 4

Spinach with Sautéed Mushrooms

3–4 bunches spinach, 2–2½ lb (1–1.25 kg)
   total weight, tough stems removed
2 or 3 pinches of salt, plus salt to taste
ground nutmeg to taste
¼ cup (2 oz/60 g) unsalted butter
½ cup (2½ oz/75 g) finely chopped
   yellow onion
1–1½ lb (500–750 g) fresh mushrooms,
   brushed clean and thickly sliced
lemon juice to taste, plus 1 lemon, cut
   into wedges

Once the spinach and mushrooms are cleaned and trimmed, this versatile side dish goes together very fast. Look for mushrooms that are white and have tightly closed caps with no dark brown gills showing.

❖❖

Place the spinach in a large saucepan with only the rinsing water that clings to the leaves. Add the 2 or 3 pinches of salt and a little nutmeg. Cover and cook over medium-high heat, turning the leaves a couple of times, until just wilted, about 2 minutes. Drain in a colander and press the leaves with the back of a spoon to remove all excess liquid. Return the spinach to the pan and fluff up the leaves. Cover partially and keep warm.

In a large sauté pan over medium heat, melt the butter. Add the onion and cook gently until translucent, about 2 minutes. Add the mushrooms, raise the heat to high, and stir and toss until just tender, 3–4 minutes. Season with salt, nutmeg, and lemon juice. Toss well.

To serve, spoon the mushrooms into the center of a warmed shallow serving dish or platter. Surround with the spinach. Garnish with the lemon wedges.

Serves 6–8

Braised Fennel in Milk

2 or 3 small fennel bulbs, about 1½ lb (750 g) total weight

¾ cup (6 fl oz/180 ml) milk

2 tablespoons unsalted butter, cut into small cubes

salt and ground pepper to taste

¼ cup (1 oz/30 g) grated Parmesan cheese

When cooked, fennel develops a delightful flavor, with only subtle hints of anise. Take care to cook the fennel just until tender. Any longer, and it can fall apart and lose its appeal.

❖

Cut off the stems and feathery tops and any bruised stalks from the fennel bulbs; save the feathery sprigs for garnish. Trim the root ends but leave the cores intact. Cut each bulb in half lengthwise and then cut each half lengthwise into 4 wedges; the portion of the core with each wedge will hold it together.

In a large sauté pan, arrange the fennel wedges, in a single layer if possible. Add the milk, dot the surface with the butter cubes, and sprinkle with salt and pepper. Bring to a simmer over medium heat, reduce the heat to medium-low, cover partially, and simmer for 15 minutes; watch carefully that the milk does not boil over. Turn the wedges over once during cooking. Uncover, raise the heat slightly, and cook until the fennel is just tender when pierced and the milk is reduced to 1–2 tablespoons, about 15 minutes longer.

Meanwhile, preheat an oven to 400°F (200°C). Butter a baking dish in which the fennel wedges will fit comfortably.

Using a spatula, carefully transfer the fennel, with its liquid, to the prepared baking dish, arranging the wedges in a single layer. Top with the Parmesan cheese. Bake until golden on top, 10–15 minutes.

To serve, chop the reserved feathery sprigs and use for garnish. Serve at once.

Serves 4

Asparagus and Beets with Romesco Mayonnaise

A spicy Catalan-inspired tomato-almond mayonnaise makes a wonderful sauce for spears of asparagus and wedges of beets.

❖❖

FOR THE ROMESCO MAYONNAISE:
1 tablespoon minced garlic
coarse salt
1½ cups (12 fl oz/375 ml) mayonnaise
1 cup (4 oz/125 g) sliced (flaked) almonds, toasted and chopped
½ cup (3 oz/90 g) seeded and finely chopped, drained canned plum (Roma) tomatoes
½ teaspoon cayenne pepper
¼ cup (2 fl oz/60 ml) tomato purée
¼ cup (2 fl oz/60 ml) red wine vinegar
salt and ground black pepper to taste

1½ lb (750 g) asparagus
12 small beets

To make the mayonnaise, in a mortar, combine the garlic with a little coarse salt and, using a pestle, grind together to form a paste. Alternatively, in a bowl, mash together with a fork or the back of a spoon. Place the mayonnaise in a bowl and stir in the garlic paste. Fold in the almonds, tomatoes, cayenne, tomato purée, vinegar, and salt and pepper until well mixed. Cover and refrigerate.

Remove the tough ends of the asparagus; trim the spears to a uniform length. If the stalks are thick, using a vegetable peeler and starting about 2 inches (5 cm) below the tips, peel off the thin outer skins.

Half fill a large, wide frying pan with salted water and bring to a boil. Add the asparagus spears and boil until tender-crisp, 4–6 minutes; the timing will depend upon the thickness of the stalks. Drain well and immerse immediately in ice water to stop the cooking and set the color. Drain well again and pat dry.

To bake the beets, preheat an oven to 375°F (190°C). Trim the greens off the beets (reserve for another use), leaving about ½ inch (12 mm) of the stems intact. Rinse the beets well but do not peel, pat dry, and wrap together in aluminum foil, sealing tightly. Place in a baking dish and add water to a depth of 1–2 inches (2.5–5 cm). Bake until tender when pierced, 45–60 minutes, depending on the size and age of the beets. Add more water as needed to make steam. Remove from the oven and let cool. Remove and discard the foil. Peel the beets and cut into wedges.

To serve, place the beets and asparagus on a platter. Pass the mayonnaise in a bowl. Serve at room temperature.

Serves 6

Grilled Vegetables with Herbed Dressing

1 tablespoon lemon juice

1 teaspoon salt, plus extra as needed

⅓ cup (3 fl oz/80 ml) extra-virgin olive oil, plus extra for brushing

1 or 2 green (spring) onions, including tender green tops, minced

1 tablespoon chopped fresh mint, oregano, basil, flat-leaf (Italian) parsley, or other herb

ground pepper to taste

2 or 3 small Asian (slender) eggplants (aubergines) or 1 small globe eggplant

2 small fennel bulbs

2 or 3 small zucchini (courgettes), cut lengthwise into slices ¼ inch (6 mm) thick

1 head radicchio, cut into 8 wedges

Almost all vegetables cook well and easily on the grill, and complement grilled meat, poultry, or fish. Offer squares of focaccia to complete the meal.

❊

*I*n a small bowl, whisk together the lemon juice and 1 teaspoon salt until the salt dissolves. Add the ⅓ cup (3 fl oz/80 ml) olive oil, green onions, mint or other herb, and pepper and whisk until blended to form a dressing. Set aside.

If using Asian eggplants, trim and cut lengthwise into slices ¼ inch (6 mm) thick. If using a globe eggplant, trim, cut in half lengthwise, and cut each half crosswise into slices ¼ inch (6 mm) thick. Sprinkle both sides of each slice lightly with salt and place in a single layer in a colander. Let stand for 45 minutes to drain off the bitter juices. Rinse the slices and pat dry with paper towels, pressing down to absorb all the moisture. Set aside.

Preheat a broiler (griller) or prepare a fire in a charcoal grill.

Cut off the stems and feathery tops and any bruised outer stalks from the fennel bulbs. Cut lengthwise into slices ⅛ inch (3 mm) thick.

Lightly brush the fennel, eggplant, and zucchini slices and radicchio wedges on both sides with olive oil. Place on a broiler pan or on a grill rack. Grill or broil, turning once, until lightly browned and tender when pierced, 4–5 minutes on each side.

Whisk the dressing again and spoon a little on the bottom of a serving platter. Arrange the vegetables on the platter and spoon a little dressing over the top. Serve warm or at room temperature. Pass any remaining dressing at the table.

Serves 4

Artichoke Hearts with Tomatoes and Currants

2 tablespoons lemon juice, or to taste, plus ½ lemon

6 large artichokes, each about 4 inches (10 cm) in diameter

¼ cup (2 fl oz/60 ml) olive oil

1 cup (8 fl oz/250 ml) water or dry white wine

2 cups (12 oz/375 g) peeled, diced tomatoes (fresh or canned)

½ cup (3 oz/90 g) dried currants, soaked in warm water to cover for 10 minutes and drained

2 tablespoons honey, plus extra to taste

salt and ground pepper to taste

Sweet-sour artichoke preparations such as this one are common in the Mediterranean, where they are enjoyed with grilled or roasted seafood, poultry, or meat.

❖❖

*H*ave ready a bowl to which you have added the 2 tablespoons lemon juice. Working with 1 artichoke at a time, cut off the stem even with the base and cut off the top third of the leaves. Break off all the tough outer leaves, then remove the remaining leaves with a small sharp knife. Rub the cut surfaces with the lemon half and add the artichoke to the lemon water. Just before cooking, drain the artichokes and pat dry.

In a large sauté pan over medium-high heat, warm the olive oil. Add the artichokes and toss to coat with the oil. Add the water or wine, cover, and cook until the artichokes are tender-crisp, 12–15 minutes; most of the liquid will have been absorbed. Add the tomatoes, currants, and 2 tablespoons honey and stir well. Simmer, uncovered, until the artichokes are tender when pierced and the pan juices have reduced, about 10 minutes longer. Season with salt and pepper. Taste and add more honey or lemon juice if desired.

Transfer the artichokes to a warmed serving platter and spoon the sauce over the tops.

Serves 6

Leeks à la Grecque

2 lb (1 kg) young, slender leeks, white
part and 1 inch (2.5 cm) of the green
1 tablespoon salt
8–10 small pearl onions
¾ cup (6 fl oz/180 ml) Chicken Stock
(*recipe on page13*) or broth or water, or
as needed
⅓ cup (3 fl oz/80 ml) dry white wine
3 tablespoons olive oil
1 tablespoon tomato paste
4 bay leaves
1 teaspoon peppercorns
paprika

*This dish goes especially well with chicken or lamb and may also be
served as a first course. Use small, tender leeks for the best results.*

❖❖

Gather the leeks together in a bundle and tie securely with
kitchen string. Fill a large, wide pot half full with water and
bring to a boil. Add the salt and the bundle of leeks and boil,
uncovered, for 5 minutes. Drain and let cool for a few minutes.
Snip the strings and set the leeks aside.

Fill a small saucepan three-fourths full with water and bring to
a boil. Using a small, sharp knife, trim off the stem and root ends
of each pearl onion, then cut a shallow X in the root ends. Add to
the pan and boil, uncovered, for 2 minutes. Drain and immerse in
cold water. Using your fingers, slip off the skins. Set aside.

In a large frying pan that will hold the leeks in a single layer,
arrange the leeks in a row. In a small bowl, stir together the ¾ cup
(6 fl oz/180 ml) stock, broth, or water; wine; olive oil; and tomato
paste. Pour the mixture over the leeks. Tuck the bay leaves under
the leeks and scatter the peppercorns over the top. Arrange the
onions among the leeks so that they sit in the liquid. The liquid
should reach just to the top of the leeks; add more stock, broth,
or water if necessary.

Place over medium heat and bring to a simmer. Reduce the
heat to low and barely simmer, uncovered, until the leeks are
tender when pierced and the liquid is reduced to a few spoonfuls,
about 45 minutes. Remove from the heat and let cool completely.

To serve, arrange the leeks in a row in a serving dish. Arrange
the onions and bay leaves over the leeks and spoon the reduced
sauce, including the peppercorns, over the leeks and onions.
Sprinkle with paprika and serve at room temperature.

Serves 4

Baked Beets with Onion and Cream

6 beets, about 3 lb (1.5 kg) total weight
2 tablespoons unsalted butter
1 white sweet onion, cut into small dice
2–3 tablespoons water
1 cup (8 fl oz/250 ml) heavy (double)
  cream
salt and ground pepper to taste
chopped fresh parsley

Baked beets have more intense taste and texture than boiled beets. This dish is an excellent companion to a simple grilled steak or chop.

❖❖

Preheat an oven to 450°F (230°C).

Trim the greens off the beets (reserve for another use), leaving about ½ inch (12 mm) of the stems intact. Rinse the beets well but do not peel. Pat dry and wrap together in aluminum foil, sealing tightly. Using a knife, make a small slit in the top of the packet for steam to escape and place in a baking pan.

Bake until tender when pierced, 45–60 minutes, depending upon the size and age of the beets. Remove from the oven and open the package partway to let the beets cool a little. Reduce the oven temperature to 375°F (190°C).

When cool enough to handle, trim and peel the beets, then cut crosswise into slices about ⅛ inch (3 mm) thick. Arrange, layered in straight rows or in concentric circles, in a baking dish.

In a sauté pan over medium-low heat, melt the butter. When foaming, add the onion and sauté gently until translucent, 6–7 minutes. Add the water, cover, and steam over low heat until the onion is tender, 8–10 minutes. Watch carefully so that the onion does not burn or brown. When the moisture has evaporated, add the cream, salt, and pepper. Raise the heat to medium, bring the cream to a boil, and cook for 1 minute. Remove from the heat and pour the cream mixture evenly over the beets. Bake, uncovered, until the sauce is bubbly, 10–15 minutes.

Sprinkle with chopped parsley and serve immediately.

Serves 4

Roasted Peppers and Eggplant

2 small eggplants (aubergines)

1 large or 2 small red (Spanish) onions, unpeeled (optional)

olive oil for rubbing on onion(s), plus ½ cup (4 fl oz/125 ml) olive oil

3 red bell peppers (capsicums)

2 teaspoons ground cumin

2 tablespoons sherry vinegar

salt and ground pepper to taste

¼ cup (⅓ oz/10 g) chopped fresh flat-leaf (Italian) parsley

handful of sharply flavored black or green olives

This versatile side dish can also be served as part of an antipasto or tapas spread. It can be assembled up to 1 day in advance; taste and adjust the seasonings before serving.

❖❖

Preheat an oven to 400°F (200°C). Place the eggplants on a baking sheet and prick all over with a fork. If using the onion(s), rub them with olive oil and add them to the baking sheet. Roast the eggplants, turning occasionally to ensure even cooking, until tender, 35–45 minutes. Set aside until cool enough to handle. Continue to roast the onion(s) until tender when pierced with a knife, about 50 minutes total, then set aside to cool.

To roast the peppers, preheat a broiler (griller). Cut the peppers in half and remove the stems, seeds, and ribs. Place, cut sides down, on a baking sheet. Broil (grill) until the skins blacken and blister. Remove from the broiler, drape the peppers loosely with aluminum foil, and let cool for 10 minutes, then peel away the skins. Cut into long, narrow strips.

Peel the eggplants and cut the flesh into 1½–2-inch (4–5-cm) cubes. Place in a colander to drain for about 30 minues. Then peel the onion(s) and cut into long, narrow strips. Set aside.

Combine the drained eggplant, bell peppers, and onion(s) in a large bowl. In a small bowl, whisk together the ½ cup (4 fl oz/125 ml) olive oil, cumin, and sherry vinegar. Add to the vegetables and toss to coat evenly. Season with salt and pepper.

Garnish with the parsley and olives, and serve.

Serves 6

Potato Latkes

1 small yellow onion
3 or 4 large russet potatoes, peeled
1 egg, beaten
1 teaspoon salt
1 teaspoon ground pepper
6–8 tablespoons (2–2½ oz/60–75 g)
  all-purpose (plain) flour
vegetable shortening (vegetable lard) or
  vegetable oil for frying

The crisp potato pancakes known as latkes are traditionally served for Hanukkah dinner, but may also be enjoyed at any other time of year with roasted meat or poultry. They are at their best with braised brisket of beef.

❈❈

*P*reheat an oven to 350°F (180°C).

Grate the onion and potatoes and place in a large bowl. Using paper towels, blot up any liquid they might have released. Stir in the egg, salt, pepper, and enough flour to bind the mixture.

In a large frying pan over high heat, add shortening or oil to a depth of 2 inches (5 cm). When the shortening or oil is hot, working in batches, drop in the batter by spoonfuls, forming cakes about 2 inches (5 cm) in diameter; be careful not to crowd the pan. Cook, turning once, until golden brown, about 3 minutes on each side. Using a spatula, transfer to paper towels to drain. Keep warm in the oven while cooking the remaining batter.

Serve as soon as the last batch is cooked; latkes will stay crisp for only a few minutes.

Makes about 12 potato pancakes; serves 6

Herbed Mashed Potatoes

6 large baking potatoes, about 3 lb
  (1.5 kg)
1 cup (8 fl oz/250 ml) heavy (double)
  cream or milk
6 tablespoons (3 oz/90 g) unsalted butter
2 teaspoons chopped fresh parsley
2 teaspoons chopped fresh thyme
2 teaspoons chopped fresh marjoram
salt and ground pepper to taste

You can use light cream, heavy cream, or milk to make this favorite side dish. And if you like the sharp flavor of buttermilk, it will work well, too, plus it is lower in fat than the other choices.

❈

Preheat an oven to 400°F (200°C).

Pierce the potatoes several times with a fork and place them directly on the oven rack or on a baking sheet. Bake until very tender, about 1 hour. Remove from the oven and let cool just until they can be handled.

While the potatoes are cooling, in a small saucepan over medium-low heat, warm the cream or milk until small bubbles form along the edges of the pan.

Cut the potatoes in half, scoop out the pulp, and pass through a potato ricer or a food mill placed over a large saucepan. Alternatively, scoop out the pulp into a bowl and mash with a potato masher, then transfer to a large saucepan.

Add the butter to the potatoes and, using a spoon or fork, mash it in. Place the pan over low heat. Stirring constantly, gradually add the hot cream or milk. Continue to stir well until the desired consistency is achieved.

Mix in the herbs and season with salt and pepper. Transfer to a warmed serving dish and serve immediately.

Serves 6–8

Potato Omelet

1 lb (500 g) baking potatoes, peeled
7 tablespoons (3½ fl oz/105 ml) water
1 tablespoon unsalted butter
3 tablespoons extra-virgin olive oil, plus extra for plate
salt to taste
1 clove garlic
2 tablespoons minced fresh parsley
6 eggs
ground pepper to taste
¼ teaspoon ground nutmeg

Flat vegetable omelets such as this one are eaten throughout southwestern Europe. Wedges of the omelet may be served alongside simple roasted meat or poultry, or as a first course.

In a food processor or with a sharp knife, cut the potatoes into matchsticks.

In a small nonstick frying pan over high heat, combine the water, butter, and 2 tablespoons of the oil. Bring to a boil and add the potatoes. Stir well and season with salt. Cover with a lid slightly ajar and cook over medium heat, turning often, until just crisp and the water evaporates, about 12 minutes. Add the garlic by passing it through a garlic press and stir in the parsley. Continue to cook, stirring, for 3 minutes.

Meanwhile, break the eggs into a large bowl. Season with salt and pepper, and add the nutmeg and the remaining 1 tablespoon oil. Beat with a fork until the eggs are completely blended. Pour the eggs over the potatoes and, when they begin to set, smooth the surface with the back of a spoon and cover the pan. Reduce the heat to low and cook for 8 minutes.

Lightly oil a plate large enough to hold the omelet. When the omelet is ready, invert it onto the oiled plate. Slide it back into the pan, browned side up, re-cover, and cook over low heat for another 8 minutes.

To serve, transfer the omelet back onto the plate. Cut into wedges and serve warm or at room temperature.

Serves 6

Baked Pork and Grape Dressing

1 loaf French bread, about 1 lb (500 g)

2 tablespoons unsalted butter, or as needed

1 lb (500 g) ground (minced) pork

2 teaspoons dried sage

1 teaspoon salt

¼ teaspoon ground black pepper

pinch of cayenne pepper

½ cup (2 oz/60 g) diced yellow onion

½ cup (2½ oz/75 g) diced celery

1 small tart apple, peeled, cored, and chopped

1 cup (6 oz/185 g) seedless green grapes, stemmed

½ cup (4 fl oz/125 ml) Chicken Stock (*recipe on page 13*) or broth

3 eggs, lightly beaten

With its pleasing combination of robust and sweet flavors, this dressing is a nice accompaniment to roast turkey and gravy. Prepare the bread crumbs well ahead of time so they dry properly.

❈

Preheat an oven to 150°F (65°C). Slice or tear the bread, including the crusts, into small pieces. Place in a food processor and process to form coarse crumbs. (You should have 8–9 cups.) Spread the crumbs on baking sheets and dry fully in the oven, about 2 hours. Do not allow to color. Let cool.

Raise the oven temperature to 350°F (180°C). Butter a 2- or 2½-qt (2- or 2.5-l) baking dish.

In a large frying pan over medium heat, melt the 2 tablespoons butter. Add the pork and stir, breaking it up with a fork, until crumbly, about 8 minutes (cook the pork in batches if the pan is not big enough to spread out the meat). Add the sage, salt, black pepper, and cayenne pepper and continue stirring and tossing until lightly browned, 4–5 minutes longer. Using a slotted spoon, transfer the meat to a plate, leaving the drippings in the pan.

Add the onion and celery to the pan, adding butter if needed, and sauté until translucent, 1–2 minutes. Add the apple and grapes and stir and toss over medium heat for 2 minutes.

Put the bread crumbs in a large bowl. In a separate bowl, stir together the stock or broth and eggs. While rapidly tossing the crumbs, gradually add the stock-egg mixture; the crumbs should be evenly moistened. Mix in the reserved meat and the apple-grape mixture. Taste and adjust the seasonings. Spoon loosely into the prepared baking dish. Bake until golden, 40–50 minutes.

Serves 6–8

Sweet Potato–Ginger Pudding

2 lb (1 kg) yellow-fleshed sweet potatoes, unpeeled

grated zest of 1 lemon

½ teaspoon salt

⅓ cup (2 oz/60 g) crystallized ginger, brushed of excess sugar and finely chopped

1½ cups (12 fl oz/375 ml) heavy (double) cream

¼ teaspoon ground nutmeg, or to taste

4 egg whites

Here is an ideal vegetable accompaniment to baked ham or turkey. The sweet potatoes can be boiled and puréed in advance and all the ingredients assembled for the final mixing and baking. If yellow sweet potatoes are not available or you prefer the orange-fleshed ones (what Americans call yams), use them.

❈

In a large saucepan, combine the sweet potatoes with water to cover. Bring to a boil, reduce the heat, cover, and cook until tender, 30–40 minutes. Drain and let cool.

Meanwhile, preheat an oven to 350°F (180°C). Butter a 2-qt (2-l) soufflé dish or baking dish.

Peel the cooled sweet potatoes, quarter, and pass through a ricer or food mill placed over a large bowl. You should have about 2½ cups (1¼ lb/625 g). Stir in the lemon zest, salt, and crystallized ginger. Then stir in the cream and nutmeg.

In a separate bowl, using an electric mixer set on medium speed, beat the egg whites until soft folds form. Add about one-fourth of the beaten whites to the potato mixture and stir in to lighten it. Then, using a rubber spatula, gently fold in the remaining whites, being careful not to deflate the mixture. Spoon into the prepared baking dish.

Bake until risen and slightly golden on top, 40–50 minutes. Serve immediately.

Serves 8–10

Mushroom-Pancetta Dressing

4 cups (8 oz/250 g) cubed day-old bread
   (about ½ loaf)
½ cup (4 oz/125 g) unsalted butter
½ lb (250 g) pancetta, cut into slices
   ¼ inch (6 mm) thick and then cut into
   strips ¼ inch (6 mm) wide
1 cup (4 oz/125 g) diced yellow onion
2 cups (6 oz/185 g) sliced mushrooms
   such as chanterelle or portobello
2 teaspoons chopped fresh thyme
2 teaspoons chopped fresh sage
½–¾ cup (4–6 fl oz/125–180 ml)
   Chicken Stock (recipe on page 13)
   or broth
salt and ground pepper to taste

If you like, loosely pack this dressing into a 6-pound (3-kg) chicken for roasting, then serve them together as the centerpiece of a special dinner.

❊❊

Preheat an oven to 300°F (150°C).

Spread the cubed bread in a large rimmed baking sheet and toast in the oven, stirring from time to time, until dried out, about 1 hour.

Meanwhile, in a large sauté pan over medium heat, melt ¼ cup (2 oz/60 g) of the butter. Add the pancetta and sauté until nearly crisp, 5–8 minutes. Using a slotted spoon, transfer the pancetta to a large bowl and set aside. To the fat remaining in the pan, add the onion and sauté over medium heat until tender and translucent, 8–10 minutes. Transfer the contents of the pan to the bowl holding the pancetta.

In the same pan over medium heat, melt the remaining ¼ cup (2 oz/60 g) butter. Add the mushrooms and sauté until they give off some liquid, about 5 minutes. Stir in the thyme and sage. Transfer the mushrooms and their juices to the bowl holding the pancetta and onion.

When the bread cubes are ready, remove from the oven and raise the oven temperature to 375°F (190°C). Butter a 2-qt (2-l) baking dish.

Add the bread cubes to the bowl and pour ½ cup (4 fl oz/ 125 ml) of the stock or broth evenly over the top. Toss until all the bread cubes are evenly moistened, adding more liquid as needed if the stuffing seems too dry. Season with salt and a generous amount of pepper. (The dressing can be covered and refrigerated for as long as overnight before cooking.)

Bake until heated through, about 45 minutes. Serve immediately.

Serves 4

Yam and Potato Gratin

3 cups (24 fl oz/750 ml) heavy (double)
   cream, or as needed
3 cloves garlic, smashed
salt and ground pepper to taste
ground nutmeg to taste
3 large russet potatoes
3 large yams

The slight edge of sweetness provided by the yams makes a particularly nice complement to barbecued chicken or any other robust, spicy-sweet main course.

❊❊

Preheat an oven to 375°F (190°C).

In a saucepan over medium-high heat, bring the 3 cups (24 fl oz/750 ml) cream and garlic to a boil. Reduce the heat to low and simmer, uncovered, for 10 minutes. Remove the garlic and discard. Season the cream with salt, pepper, and nutmeg. The mixture should be a little salty, as the potatoes are very bland and will absorb the cream and salt.

While the cream is simmering, peel the potatoes and yams and slice ¼ inch (6 mm) thick. In a deep baking dish, arrange the slices in overlapping rows. Pour the hot cream over the slices. It should just cover the them; if not, add more as needed.

Bake until the potatoes and yams are tender when pierced, about 45 minutes. Serve at once.

Serves 6

Celery Root and Potato Purée

4 large baking potatoes
2 celery roots, peeled and diced
1½–2 cups (12–16 fl oz/375–500 ml)
   Chicken Stock *(recipe on page 13)*
   or broth
3 tablespoons unsalted butter, or as
   needed
½ cup (4 fl oz/125 ml) heavy (double)
   cream, or as needed
salt and ground pepper to taste
ground nutmeg to taste

At a gala dinner, replace your regular mashed potatoes with this distinctive side dish. The celery root gives the purée a subtle edge of sweetness and lightness.

❋

Preheat an oven to 400°F (200°C).

Pierce the potatoes in several places with a fork and place them on the oven rack or on a baking sheet. Bake until very tender, about 1 hour.

While the potatoes are baking, in a saucepan, combine the celery roots with enough stock or broth to cover. Place over low heat and cook, uncovered, until very tender, about 25 minutes. Drain and purée in a food processor or pass through a food mill placed over a heavy saucepan.

When the potatoes are ready, remove from the oven. When cool enough to handle, cut in half, scoop out the pulp, and pass through a ricer or food mill placed over the saucepan holding the celery root. Place the saucepan over medium heat and stir in the 3 tablespoons butter and ½ cup (4 fl oz/125 ml) cream. Heat to serving temperature, stirring often to prevent scorching. If necessary, add more butter and cream or stock or broth to achieve a thick, smooth consistency.

Season with salt, pepper, and a little nutmeg. Spoon into a warmed serving dish and serve at once.

Serves 4

Mixed Bean Pot with Pancetta

1 cup (7 oz/220 g) dried red kidney
  beans

1 cup (7 oz/220 g) dried small white
  (navy) beans

1 cup (7 oz/220 g) dried chickpeas
  (garbanzo beans)

2 cups (16 fl oz/500 ml) Chicken Stock
  (*recipe on page 13*) or broth

1 tablespoon olive oil

¼ lb (125 g) pancetta, chopped

2 yellow onions, sliced

3 cloves garlic, minced

1 teaspoon dried thyme

1 teaspoon dried sage

3-inch (7.5-cm) strip orange zest pierced
  with 4 whole cloves

1 can (14½ oz/455 g) chopped tomatoes,
  with their juices

1–2 teaspoons salt

ground pepper to taste

1 cup (2 oz/60 g) fresh bread crumbs
  tossed with 2 tablespoons melted
  unsalted butter

1 fresh sage sprig

Hearty and flavorful, these baked beans seem made to serve alongside grilled sausages. Or offer them on their own for a casual, satisfying cold-weather supper.

※

Pick over all the beans and discard any misshapen beans or stones. Rinse the beans and drain. Place in a bowl, add water to cover generously, and let soak for 3 hours. Drain the beans and place in a saucepan. Add the stock or broth and then hot water to cover by 1 inch (2.5 cm). Bring to a boil, reduce the heat to low, cover, and simmer gently until tender, about 1 hour; the timing will depend upon the size and age of the beans.

Preheat an oven to 350°F (180°C).

In a large sauté pan over medium heat, warm the olive oil. Add the pancetta and sauté until lightly cooked, about 5 minutes. Using a slotted spoon, transfer to a small bowl. Add the onions, garlic, thyme, and sage to the same pan, cover, and cook over medium-low heat until soft, 6–7 minutes. Uncover and stir in the beans and their liquid, pancetta, orange zest with cloves, and tomatoes with juices. Season with salt and pepper. Raise the heat to medium-high and bring to a boil.

Transfer the bean mixture to a deep baking dish. Top with the buttered bread crumbs. Bake until browned, about 30 minutes. Garnish with the sage sprig and serve piping hot.

Serves 6–8

Saffron Rice

2 cups (14 oz/440 g) basmati rice
6 qt (6 l) water
salt to taste
¼ cup (2 fl oz/60 ml) dry white wine or water
1 teaspoon saffron threads
4–6 tablespoons (2–3 oz/60–90 g) unsalted butter
1 cinnamon stick
8 whole cloves
seeds from 8 cardamom pods
ground pepper to taste

Raisins or almonds are a good addition to this rice dish, an aromatic partner for curries. Soak ½ cup (3 oz/90 g) raisins in hot water to cover until soft and plump, about 20 minutes, then drain and add to the butter with the spices. Or add ½ cup (2½ oz/75 g) chopped toasted almonds to the butter with the spices.

In a bowl, combine the rice and water to cover by 1 inch (2.5 cm). Let stand for 2 hours; drain. Preheat an oven to 350°F (180°C).

In a saucepan, bring the 6 qt (6 l) water to a boil and add the salt. Add the drained rice and boil for 10 minutes. Drain the rice and rinse with warm water. Drain again and place in a shallow 1½-qt (1.5-l) baking dish measuring about 9 by 11 by 2 inches (23 by 28 by 5 cm).

Meanwhile, in a small pan over low heat, warm the wine or water; remove from the heat. Crush the saffron threads gently and add to the warm liquid. Let stand for 10 minutes.

In a small sauté pan or saucepan over medium heat, melt the butter. Add the saffron and its soaking liquid, cinnamon, cloves, cardamom, and pepper and toss with the butter. Add the butter mixture to the rice, toss well, and then cover the baking dish with aluminum foil.

Bake until the butter has been absorbed and the rice is tender but still firm, about 25 minutes. Remove the cinnamon stick and cloves and discard. Serve immediately.

Serves 6

Polenta with Tomato Sauce

2 tablespoons olive oil

1 yellow onion, chopped

3 cloves garlic, minced

3 cups (18 oz/560 g) peeled, seeded, and chopped tomatoes, with their juices (fresh or canned)

3–4 tablespoons tomato paste

2 teaspoons sugar

1 tablespoon chopped fresh basil

½ teaspoon ground pepper

salt to taste, plus 1 tablespoon

6½ cups (52 fl oz/1.6 l) water

2 cups (10 oz/315 g) polenta or coarse yellow cornmeal

olive oil, if frying the polenta

2 oz (60 g) thinly sliced prosciutto, coarsely chopped

fresh basil sprigs (optional)

grated Parmesan cheese

Serve the polenta directly from the saucepan in warmed individual bowls, or spread the hot polenta on an oiled baking sheet, let it cool until set, cut into squares, and fry in olive oil. The simple tomato sauce is a delicious topping in either case.

❈

*I*n a heavy-bottomed saucepan over medium heat, warm the olive oil. Add the onion and garlic and sauté, stirring, until translucent, 5–6 minutes. Stir in the tomatoes, tomato paste, sugar, basil, pepper, and salt to taste. Bring to a boil, reduce the heat to low, and simmer, uncovered, until thickened, 30–40 minutes.

Meanwhile, in a deep, heavy saucepan over high heat, bring the water to a boil. Add the 1 tablespoon salt and reduce the heat to low so the water simmers. Stirring constantly, add the polenta or cornmeal in a thin, steady stream. Cook, stirring with a wooden spoon, until the polenta is thick and creamy and begins to pull away from the pan sides, about 20 minutes.

If soft polenta is preferred, simply spoon the polenta into warmed shallow bowls.

If polenta squares are preferred, have ready an oiled rimmed baking sheet. Pour the hot polenta into it, forming a layer ½ inch (12 mm) thick and smoothing the top. Cover with plastic wrap and refrigerate until firm, about 12 hours. Then cut into squares. In a large frying pan over high heat, pour in olive oil to a depth of ½ inch (12 mm). When the oil is hot, working in batches, fry the squares, turning once, until crispy but not browned, 4–6 minutes total. Transfer to warmed individual bowls or plates.

Reheat the tomato sauce, if necessary, and spoon it over the hot soft polenta or polenta squares. Scatter the prosciutto over the top and garnish with the basil, if using, and the Parmesan cheese.

Serves 4–6

Baked Semolina Gnocchi

4 cups (32 fl oz/1 l) milk
½ teaspoon salt
ground pepper to taste
pinch of ground nutmeg
1 cup (6 oz/185 g) semolina flour
1 tablespoon unsalted butter, plus ¼ cup
   (2 oz/60 g), melted
⅔ cup (2½ oz/74 g) grated Parmesan
   cheese
2 egg yolks, lightly beaten

The gnocchi can be made in advance and refrigerated; just slip the dish in the oven 15 minutes before serving.

❉

In a deep, heavy saucepan over medium heat, warm the milk until small bubbles appear along the edges of the pan; do not allow to boil. Add the salt, pepper, and nutmeg. Stirring constantly with a heavy whisk or wooden spoon, slowly pour in the semolina. Reduce the heat to low and continue to cook, stirring, until the mixture is very thick and stiff, 10–12 minutes.

Remove from the heat and add the 1 tablespoon butter; stir until fully melted. Stir in ⅓ cup (1¼ oz/37 g) of the Parmesan cheese until combined. Add the egg yolks and stir vigorously until well blended and smooth.

Wet a jelly-roll (Swiss-roll) pan or a 10-by-15-inch (25-by-38-cm) baking pan with cold water. Using a wet spatula or spoon, spread the semolina mixture evenly in the pan. It should be about ¼ inch (6 mm) thick. Let cool completely until set, 40–50 minutes.

Preheat an oven to 425°F (220°C). Generously butter a round 10-inch (25-cm) baking dish or a 9-by-11-inch (23-by-28-cm) rectangular or oval baking dish.

Using a round cutter 1½–2 inches (4–5 cm) in diameter, cut out rounds of the firm semolina. Place in a single layer in the prepared baking dish, overlapping them slightly. Gather up the scraps, cut out additional rounds, and add to the dish. Using a spoon, distribute the melted butter evenly over the rounds. Sprinkle the remaining ⅓ cup (1¼ oz/37 g) cheese evenly over the top.

Bake until the top is golden and the butter is bubbly, about 15 minutes. Transfer the gnocchi to warmed plates and serve.

Serves 4

Flageolet Beans with Cream

1½ cups (10½ oz/330 g) dried flageolet
  beans
2 fresh thyme sprigs
2 fresh parsley sprigs
1 bay leaf
1 celery stalk, cut crosswise into 4 equal
  pieces
1 small white sweet onion, stuck with
  2 whole cloves
½ teaspoon salt, plus salt to taste
1 tablespoon sour cream
1½–2 teaspoons Dijon mustard
½–¾ cup (4–6 fl oz/125–180 ml) heavy
  (double) cream
2 teaspoons chopped fresh tarragon, plus
  extra to taste, if needed
ground pepper to taste

Prepared in this way, flageolets, which are small, pale green kidney-shaped beans, are delicious alongside grilled lamb, chicken, or fish. You can also serve them on their own as a warm first course.

❈

Pick over the beans and discard any misshapen beans or stones. Rinse the beans and drain. Place in a large bowl, add water to cover generously, and let soak for 3 hours.

Drain the beans and place in a saucepan with water to cover by 1 inch (2.5 cm). Place the thyme and parsley sprigs and bay leaf inside the celery pieces and tie securely with kitchen string to form a bouquet garni. Add to the pan along with the clove-studded onion and ½ teaspoon salt. Bring to a boil over medium-high heat, reduce the heat to low, cover partially, and simmer gently until the beans are tender, 30–45 minutes; the timing will depend upon the size and age of the beans.

Remove and discard the herb bouquet and onion. Let cool for 10 minutes, then drain the beans and return them to the pan. In a small bowl, combine the sour cream and mustard to taste and mix well. Add the heavy cream to taste, stir until well blended, and then stir in 1 teaspoon of the tarragon. Add the cream mixture to the beans, stir gently to blend, and place over medium-low heat. Warm gently to serving temperature. Season to taste with salt, pepper, and more mustard, cream, or tarragon if needed. Do not stir too much or the beans will become mushy.

Transfer to a warmed serving dish or spoon onto warmed plates. Sprinkle evenly with the remaining 1 teaspoon tarragon and serve immediately.

Serves 4

Rice Pilaf

2 tablespoons peanut oil or olive oil

1 yellow onion, diced

2 cups (14 oz/440 g) basmati or jasmine
  rice, rinsed and drained

4 cups (32 fl oz/1 l) water or Chicken
  Stock *(recipe on page 13)* or broth

1 piece fresh ginger, 1½–2 inches
  (4–5 cm) long, peeled and smashed

salt to taste

Here is a classic rice pilaf that may be embellished. Among the possibilities are ¼ cup (1¼ oz/37 g) toasted pine nuts or almonds; ¼ cup (1½ oz/45 g) dried currants, soaked in hot water to cover for 20 minutes and drained; 6 tablespoons (1 oz/30 g) minced green (spring) onion tops; 1 small tomato, peeled, seeded, and diced; and/or 2 tablespoons lightly toasted flaked dried coconut. Stir in one or more additions just before removing the pan from the heat.

❋

*I*n a saucepan over medium heat, warm the oil. Add the onion and sauté until translucent and tender, 8–10 minutes. Add the rice and sauté for a few minutes until the grains are thoroughly coated with the oil.

Add the water or other liquid, ginger, and salt and bring to a boil. Cook for 2 minutes, reduce the heat to low, cover, and simmer until the water is absorbed and the rice is tender, 15–20 minutes.

Remove from the heat and let stand, covered, for 10 minutes. Then fluff with a fork, remove the ginger, and serve at once.

Serves 4

Couscous with Roasted Winter Vegetables

FOR THE VEGETABLES:

½ small butternut squash, ¾ lb (375 g)

2 yellow onions

2 rutabagas or turnips, or one of each

2 parsnips

2 carrots

10 or more large cloves garlic

¼ cup (⅓ oz/10 g) chopped fresh sage

3 tablespoons olive oil

1 teaspoon salt

½ teaspoon ground pepper

FOR THE COUSCOUS:

2¼ cups (18 fl oz/560 ml) Vegetable
   Stock (*recipe on page 12*) or Chicken
   Stock (*recipe on page 13*) or broth

1⅓ cups (8 oz/250 g) instant couscous

salt and ground pepper to taste

Oven roasting, an easy cooking method, brings out the full flavor of the vegetables. Serve with brothy stews of poultry or seafood, or with roasts.

❋

Preheat an oven to 425°F (220°C). Coat a large roasting pan with nonstick cooking spray.

As you prepare each of the following vegetables, add it to the pan: Scrape out the seeds from the squash, then, using a vegetable peeler, peel away the skin. Cut the flesh into 1-inch (2.5-cm) cubes. Peel the onions and cut each into 8 wedges. Peel the rutabagas or turnips and cut into 1-inch (2.5-cm) chunks or cubes. Peel the parsnips and carrots, halve them lengthwise, and then cut crosswise into 1-inch (2.5-cm) pieces. Add the garlic, sage, oil, salt, and pepper to the vegetables. Stir and toss to combine and coat the vegetables evenly.

Bake, stirring occasionally, until the vegetables are lightly browned and tender when pierced, 45–55 minutes.

When the vegetables are nearly done, prepare the couscous: In a saucepan, bring the stock or broth to a boil. Stir in the couscous, cover, and remove from the heat. Set aside for 5 minutes. Fluff with a fork and season to taste with salt and pepper.

To serve, mound the couscous on a warmed platter. Spoon the roasted vegetables on top and serve at once.

Serves 4

Polenta with Pesto

FOR THE POLENTA:

1½ cups (12 fl oz/375 ml) water

1½ cups (12 fl oz/375 ml) nonfat milk

1 tablespoon unsalted butter

1 teaspoon salt

pinch of red pepper flakes

¾ cup (4 oz/125 g) polenta or coarse
yellow cornmeal

FOR THE PESTO:

3 cups (3 oz/90 g) loosely packed fresh
basil leaves

½ cup (½ oz/15 g) fresh flat-leaf (Italian)
parsley sprigs or 1 cup (1 oz/30 g) fresh
curly-leaf parsley sprigs

2 large cloves garlic

¼ cup (2 fl oz/60 ml) olive oil

½ teaspoon salt

¼ cup (1 oz/30 g) grated Parmesan
cheese

With its robust texture, polenta has a natural affinity for a variety of toppings and sauces. Sliced and browned, it makes a delicious base for pesto or tomato sauce, or for grilled chicken or fish.

❈

Coat a 9-inch (23-cm) round pie pan with nonstick cooking spray.

To make the polenta, in a saucepan over high heat, combine the water, milk, butter, salt, and pepper flakes and bring to a boil. Reduce the heat to low so the water simmers. Stirring constantly, add the polenta or cornmeal in a thin, steady stream. Cook, stirring with a wooden spoon, until the polenta is thick and creamy and begins to pull away from the pan sides, about 20 minutes. Pour the hot polenta into the prepared pie pan and smooth the top. Cover with plastic wrap and refrigerate until firm, about 12 hours.

Meanwhile, make the pesto: In a food processor, combine the basil, parsley, and garlic. Process until puréed. With the motor running, add the olive oil in a thin, steady stream. Add the salt and cheese and process until smooth. If the pesto seems too thick, add 1–2 tablespoons water. You should have at least ¾ cup (6 fl oz/180 ml). Set aside.

Cut the polenta into 8 wedges and, using a spatula, remove from the pie pan. Coat a large nonstick frying pan with nonstick cooking spray and place over medium-high heat. When hot, add the polenta wedges and cook, turning once, until lightly browned, about 3 minutes on each side.

To serve, transfer the wedges to a warmed platter or individual plates. Spoon half of the pesto over the wedges. Pass the remaining pesto at the table.

Serves 4

Spiced Apricot Chutney

This sweet-tart chutney complements lamb in particular, although it also is a delectable accompaniment to roasted chicken.

❧❧

6 cups (1½ lb/750 g) pitted and quartered fresh apricots

2 cups (1 lb/500 g) sugar

1½ teaspoons salt

1 onion, chopped

1 piece fresh ginger, 4 inches (10 cm) long, peeled and sliced

3 cloves garlic

1 teaspoon ground cinnamon

½ teaspoon ground cloves

½ teaspoon cayenne pepper or 3 or 4 jalapeño chiles, seeded, if desired, and minced

1½ cups (12 fl oz/360 ml) cider vinegar

Place the apricots in a large, heavy nonaluminum pot. Cover with the sugar and salt and let stand for at least 1 hour or for up to 8 hours.

In a food processor or blender, combine the onion, ginger, garlic, cinnamon, cloves, and cayenne or chiles. Pulse until chopped. Add ¾ cup (6 fl oz/180 ml) of the vinegar and purée until smooth. Pour over the apricots and stir in the remaining ¾ cup (6 fl oz/180 ml) vinegar. Bring to a boil, reduce the heat to low, and simmer uncovered, stirring often, until the mixture is thick and a teaspoonful dropped onto a chilled plate sets up on contact, about 1 hour.

Remove from the heat and serve warm or at room temperature. Store any leftovers in a covered jar in the refrigerator for up to 2 weeks.

Makes about 3 cups (1½ lb/750 g)

Cranberry-Tangerine Conserve

finely grated zest of 3 or 4 tangerines

2 cups (16 fl oz/500 ml) tangerine juice

1½ cups (12 oz/375 g) sugar

½ teaspoon ground ginger

½ teaspoon ground cinnamon

4 cups (1 lb/500 g) cranberries

It doesn't have to be a holiday to serve a tangy cranberry conserve to accompany roasted meat or poultry. Frozen cranberries can be found throughout the year. The conserve can be made up to 4 days in advance, covered, and stored in the refrigerator.

In a saucepan over high heat, combine the tangerine zest, 1½ cups (12 fl oz/375 ml) of the tangerine juice, sugar, ginger, and cinnamon. Bring to a boil, stirring to dissolve the sugar. Reduce the heat to medium and simmer, uncovered, for 10 minutes. Add the cranberries and cook until the berries pop and the mixture starts to bubble, 5–7 minutes longer.

Stir in the remaining ½ cup (4 fl oz/125 ml) tangerine juice and continue to simmer, stirring occasionally, until the cranberries are very tender and the juices are syrupy but not too thick, 10–15 minutes. The syrup will continue to thicken as the conserve cools.

Pour into a bowl and let cool. Store any leftovers in a covered jar in the refrigerator for up to 2 weeks.

Makes about 6 cups (3 lb/1.5 kg)

Apricot Mustard

1 cup (3 oz/90 g) dry mustard

½ cup (4 fl oz/125 ml) cider vinegar

1 cup (6 oz/185 g) dried apricots

1 cup (8 fl oz/250 ml) hot water, or as
    needed to cover

½ cup (4 fl oz/125 ml) orange juice

1 cup (7 oz/220 g) firmly packed dark
    brown sugar

½ teaspoon salt

½ teaspoon ground cinnamon

¼ teaspoon ground ginger

This flavorful mustard marries well with roast pork loin or grilled sausages. Serve it at the table for eating along with the meat, or slather it on fresh rolls or bread for building tasty sandwiches.

❧

In a bowl, whisk together the dry mustard and vinegar. Let stand for 1 hour. Meanwhile, in a small saucepan, combine the apricots and the water. Let stand for 30 minutes.

Place the pan with the apricots and water over medium heat, bring to a simmer, and cook, uncovered, until the apricots have fully softened, about 5 minutes. Remove from the heat.

In a food processor, combine the apricots and any liquid remaining in the pan and the orange juice. Purée until smooth. Add the mustard-vinegar mixture, brown sugar, salt, cinnamon, and ginger. Process until well mixed.

Transfer to a container, cover tightly, and refrigerate until serving time or for up to 2 weeks.

Makes about 3 cups (1½ lb/750 g)

Cranberry Chutney

2 cups (16 fl oz/500 ml) water

3 cups (1½ lb/750 g) sugar

2 oranges, unpeeled, seeded, and finely
chopped

2 pieces fresh ginger, each 2 inches
(5 cm) long, peeled and thinly sliced

4 cups (1 lb/500 g) cranberries

1 teaspoon ground cinnamon

½ teaspoon ground cloves

1 cup (6 oz/185 g) raisins

Serve this raisin-laced chutney with your next holiday roasted turkey. It is also good as a condiment on leftover-turkey sandwiches.

❧

*I*n a deep saucepan over high heat, combine the water and sugar. Bring to a boil, stirring to dissolve the sugar. Add the oranges and ginger, reduce the heat to low, and simmer, uncovered, until the oranges have softened, about 20 minutes. Add the cranberries, cinnamon, and cloves and cook, uncovered, until the cranberries pop and the mixture thickens, about 15 minutes.

Stir in the raisins and cook until big bubbles appear, about 7 minutes. Pour into a bowl and let cool. Serve at room temperature. Store any leftovers in a covered jar in the refrigerator for up to 2 weeks.

Makes about 6 cups (3 lb/1.5 kg)

Glossary

The following glossary defines terms both generally and as they relate specifically to their use in side dishes, including major and unusual ingredients and basic techniques.

ANCHOVIES
These tiny saltwater fish, related to the sardine, add intense, briny flavor to salads and other vegetable side dishes. They are usually sold as canned fillets that have been salted and packed in oil. Imported fillets in olive oil are the best choice for the recipes in this book.

ARTICHOKES
The flower buds of a type of thistle native to the Mediterranean. Their cluster of tough, pointed leaves covers pale green inner leaves and a prickly, inedible choke that tops a tender, gray-green base.

BEETS
Root vegetable with a round bulb and long, dark green stalks and leaves. The most common variety is a deep purplish red; others have yellowish orange, orange, or white and red flesh. Both the bulb and the greens are edible.

BELGIAN ENDIVE
A leaf vegetable with refreshing, slightly bitter, spear-shaped leaves that are white to pale yellow-green—or sometimes red—in color and tightly packed in cylindrical heads 4–6 inches (10–15 cm) long. Also known as chicory or witloof.

BREAD CRUMBS, FRESH
Fresh bread crumbs add body to vegetable dishes and are used to make a crusty topping for stuffed vegetables and other side dishes.

To make crumbs, select a good-quality coarse country bread made of unbleached wheat flour, with a firm, coarse-textured crumb. Cut away the crusts and crumble the bread by hand or in a blender or a food processor fitted with the metal blade.

BRUSSELS SPROUTS
Small, spherical green vegetables, usually 1–2 inches (2.5–5 cm) in diameter. They resemble tiny cabbages, to which they are related.

BUTTERNUT SQUASH
A pale, yellowish tan winter squash with yellow to orange flesh. Commonly 8–12 inches (20–30 cm) long, it has a broad, bulblike base and an elongated neck. In season from early summer to late autumn. Enjoyed baked and puréed or cut into chunks and roasted.

CAPERS
The small buds of a Mediterranean bush, capers are most commonly pickled in salt and vinegar and used to flavor or garnish salads and an array of vegetable side dishes. Capers should be rinsed well and drained before using.

CELERY ROOT
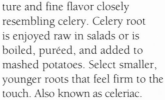
Large, knobby root of a species of celery plant, with a crisp texture and fine flavor closely resembling celery. Celery root is enjoyed raw in salads or is boiled, puréed, and added to mashed potatoes. Select smaller, younger roots that feel firm to the touch. Also known as celeriac.

CHEESE
Many different cheeses are used to flavor and garnish salads and other vegetable side dishes. Among those used in this book are blue cheese, a strong-flavored cheese marked with blue veins; commonly available varieties include Gorgonzola, Maytag, Roquefort, and Stilton. Gruyère is a smooth, firm-textured cow's milk cheese with a subtly nutty flavor. Parmesan (below), a hard, thick-crusted cow's milk cheese, is prized for its sharp, salty, full flavor. For the best quality,

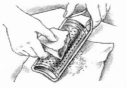

purchase Parmesan in block form and grate fresh as needed.

CHILI POWDER
A commercial blend of spices featuring ground dried chiles and also including cumin, oregano, cloves, and coriander. Purchase in small quantities, as its flavor diminishes rapidly after opening.

COCONUT MILK
Although often thought to be the liquid found inside whole coconuts, coconut milk is an extract made from shredded fresh coconut. It is sold in Asian markets and well-stocked food stores. Coconut milk is used to lend a rich sweetness to vegetable side dishes and curries.

COUSCOUS
Small, granular particles of semolina pasta that, when cooked, have a fluffy consistency resembling rice pilaf. Popular as a side dish or as a foundation for roasted vegetables or stews, couscous is often considered a grain rather than a pasta. Quick-cooking couscous has been pre-cooked and then redried; it cooks in minutes, whereas traditional couscous takes as long as 1½ hours to steam.

CURRANTS, DRIED

Produced from a variety of small grape, dried currants resemble tiny raisins but have a stronger, tastier flavor. If currants are unavailable, raisins may be substituted.

CURRY POWDER
Generic term for blends of spices commonly used to flavor Indian-style dishes. Most blends contain coriander, cumin, ground chile, fenugreek, and turmeric. Some may also include cardamom, cinnamon, cloves, allspice, fennel seeds, and ginger.

DIJON MUSTARD

One of many mustards produced in France, Dijon mustard is made in and around the city of Dijon from dark brown mustard seeds (or from light seeds and marked *blanc*) and white wine or wine vinegar. Both Dijon mustard and non-French blends labeled Dijon style are fairly sharp tasting.

EGGPLANTS

Mildly earthy, sweet vegetable-fruits with creamy white flesh and a tough, shiny skin, which may be peeled or left intact in grilled or long-cooked dishes. The skin varies in color from purple to red to white. The purple globe eggplant is the most common variety. Also available is the slender, purple Asian egg-

plant (above), which has a more tender flesh and fewer, smaller seeds. Baby eggplants of both varieties can be found in produce markets and well-stocked food stores. Also known as aubergine.

ENGLISH PEAS

Also called green peas, these shelled peas have a sweet flavor and tender texture. When purchasing fresh peas, choose pods that are plump and bright green.

FENNEL

Bulb vegetable with a crisp, refreshing, mildly anise flavor, used raw in salads and cooked by such methods as braising and grilling. The fine, feathery leaves are used as a fresh or dried herb.

GINGER

The knobby rhizome of the tropical ginger plant. Whole ginger rhizomes, commonly but mistakenly called roots, are usually purchased fresh. Peeled before use, fresh ginger adds a pungent, spicy flavor to rice pilaf, rice salad, chutneys, and other side dishes. Crystallized, or candied, ginger is made by first preserving pieces of ginger in sugar syrup and then coating them with granulated sugar.

GREEN BEANS

Also known as string beans or snap beans, these fresh beans are picked when their pods and the seeds inside are immature, still tender, and edible. The Blue Lake variety and the small French haricots verts are particularly favored for their bright color and crisp texture. Green beans are steamed or blanched and combined with other vegetables in side dishes served hot or cold.

HONEY

This sweet, syruplike substance is produced by bees from flower nectar. Each type of honey subtly reflects the color, taste, and aroma of the blossoms from which it was made. Milder varieties, such as clover and orange blossom, are lighter in color and better suited to general cooking. Those derived from herb blossoms, such as thyme, have a more distinctively aromatic taste.

HERBS

All manner of herbs, both fresh and dried, enhance the flavor of vegetable, bean, and grain side dishes. Among the most common types, used in this book, are:

Basil Sweet, spicy herb popular in Italian and French cooking, particularly as a seasoning for tomatoes.

Bay leaves Dried whole leaves of the bay laurel tree. They add a pungent and spicy flavor to stocks and other simmered dishes. The French variety has a milder, sweeter flavor than California bay leaves.

Cilantro Green, leafy herb resembling flat-leaf (Italian) parsley, with a sharp, somewhat astringent flavor. Also known as fresh coriander or Chinese parsley.

Dill Herb with fine, feathery leaves and a sweet, aromatic flavor. Used fresh or dried.

Oregano Pungent, spicy Mediterranean herb, popular in dishes featuring tomatoes and other vegetables. Also known as wild marjoram.

Parsley A popular herb available in two main varieties. Flat-leaf parsley, also known as Italian parsley, is preferred for its pronounced flavor. This and the curly-leaf type (above) are commonly available fresh in most food stores.

Rosemary A member of the mint family with strong-flavored, needlelike leaves.

Sage Pungent herb used fresh or dried in many poultry dressings and stuffings.

Tarragon Fragrant herb with a distinctive sweetness.

Thyme Fragrant, clean-tasting, small-leaved herb, available fresh or dried. A variety called lemon thyme has a subtle lemon scent and taste.

Crushing Dried Herbs

If using dried herbs, it is best to crush them first in the palm of the hand to release their flavor.

Alternatively, warm the herbs in a dry frying pan and crush using a mortar and pestle.

MARSALA
Amber Italian wine, dry or sweet in flavor, from the area of Marsala, in Sicily.

MUSHROOMS
The meaty texture and rich, earthy flavor of mushrooms make them ideal for use in dressings that accompany poultry and in vegetable side dishes.

Cultivated White Mushroom
Common variety with white caps and white stems, readily available in food stores and greengrocers. The smallest white mushrooms, with their caps still closed, are often called button mushrooms.

Chanterelle
Usually pale yellow, trumpet-shaped mushroom, 2–3 inches (5–7.5 cm) long, with a subtle flavor. Chanterelles grow in the wild and are also cultivated commercially.

Portobello Mature form of the cremini mushroom, with large, dark brown caps, 4–6 inches (10–15 cm) in diameter. Portobellos are appreciated for their particularly robust texture.

NUTS
An array of nuts are used to add crisp, crunchy texture to salads and to side dishes featuring vegetables and grains.

Almonds Mellow, sweet, oval-shaped nuts that are an important crop in California and are popular throughout the world. Sold whole (with their skins intact) and blanched (with their skins removed) and thinly sliced (flaked).

Hazelnuts Small, usually spherical nuts with a slightly sweet flavor. Also known as filberts.

Pine Nuts Small, ivory seeds from the cones of a species of pine tree and possessing a rich, subtly resinous flavor.

Walnuts Rich, crisp nuts (below) with distinctively crinkled surfaces. English walnuts are the most familiar variety; the largest crops are in California.

To toast nuts, which brings out their full flavor and aroma, spread the nuts in a single layer on a baking sheet and toast in a preheated 325° F (165° C) oven until they just begin to change color and are fragrant, 5–10 minutes. Remove from the oven and let cool to room temperature.

Toasting such nuts as hazelnuts also loosens the skins, which may be removed by wrapping the still-warm nuts in a kitchen towel and rubbing against them with the palms of your hands.

OLIVE OILS
The most flavorful olive oil is extra virgin, extracted from olives on the first pressing without use of heat or chemicals, and prized for its pure, fruity taste and golden to pale green hue. Products labeled "pure olive oil" are milder in aroma and flavor and may be used for all-purpose cooking.

OLIVES
These small fruits of trees native to the Mediterranean and cultivated in other regions are cured and sold by the pound or in bottles or cans. For the best results for use in salad, vegetable, grain, and other side dishes, seek out Mediterranean-style black or green olives cured in brine or

salt, and packed in vinegar or oil with other seasonings. Among the varieties available in food stores and delicatessens are the small, salt-cured Gaeta; the brine-cured, vinegar-packed Kalamata; the small, black, salt-cured Niçoise (above), and the sun-dried, oil-cured Moroccan.

PANCETTA
An unsmoked bacon that has been cured simply with salt and pepper. It is available in Italian delicatessens and well-stocked food stores.

PARSNIPS
Similar in shape and texture to the carrot, this root vegetable has ivory flesh and an appealingly sweet flavor. Choose firm parsnips with unblemished flesh. Generally cooked by roasting, boiling, sautéing, or steaming.

POLENTA
Italian term for a cooked mush of specially ground cornmeal and for the cornmeal itself. Cooked polenta is sometimes enriched with butter, cream, or cheese, and is often served as a side dish with a savory sauce or topping.

PROSCIUTTO
A raw ham that is cured by dry-salting for 1 month, then air-drying in cool curing sheds for 6 months or longer. A specialty of Parma, Italy, it is often cut into tissue-thin slices that emphasize its deep pink color and intense flavor. Look for prosciutto in Italian delicatessens and well-stocked food stores.

RADICCHIO
The most common variety of this type of chicory has small reddish purple leaves with pronounced white ribs, formed into a sphere. Other varieties are slightly tapered and vary in color. Enjoyed raw and cooked.

RICE
A versatile grain used as popular side dish to accompany a wide range of main courses, from vegetable stews to meat and poultry.

Basmati Long-grain white variety, principally from India, which cooks to form fluffy individual grains prized for their highly aromatic character.

Jasmine An aromatic white rice from Thailand used in pilafs and to accompany Asian dishes.

Wild Despite its name, actually a grain native to Minnesota and cultivated in other regions. The unpolished dark brown kernels have a rich nutlike flavor and appealing texture.

RUTABAGAS

Root vegetables resembling turnips, with sweet, pale yellow-orange flesh. Rutabagas are commonly enjoyed roasted, and boiled or steamed and puréed. Also known as swedes or Swedish turnips.

SEMOLINA FLOUR

Flour made from durum wheat and used to make gnocchi and other Italian specialties. Seek out in Italian delicatessens and well-stocked food stores.

SESEAME OILS, ASIAN

Sesame oils from China and Japan are commonly made with roasted sesame seeds, resulting in dark, strong-tasting oils generally used as a flavoring. Their low smoking point makes them unsuitable for using alone as a cooking medium.

SHALLOTS

Small member of the onion family with brownish skin and white flesh tinged with purple. The flavor resembles a cross between sweet onion and garlic. Minced and sautéed, shallots are added to salads, poultry dressings, and other vegetable side dishes.

TURNIPS

Creamy white root vegetable, tinged purple or green at its crown, with firm, pungent yet slightly sweet flesh. Usually cooked by roasting, boiling, or steaming. Choose smaller turnips that feel heavy for their size and are firm to the touch.

VINEGARS

Literally "sour wine," vinegar results when certain strains of yeast cause wine—or some other alcoholic liquid such as apple cider—to ferment for a second time and turn acidic. The best wine vinegars begin with good-quality wine. Red wine vinegar, like the wine from which it is produced, has a more robust flavor than vinegar made from white wine. Sherry vinegar has a rich flavor and color reminiscent of the fortified, cask-aged aperitif wine. Flavored vinegars are made by adding herbs such as tarragon.

ZUCCHINI

Slender and tube shaped, this variety of squash has edible green, yellow, or green-and-cream-striped skin and pale, tender flesh. Also known as summer squash or courgette. Look for

smaller-sized squashes, which have a finer texture and flavor and less-pronounced seeds than most larger specimens. Used raw or cooked in salads and other side dishes.

SPICES

Many different spices are used to flavor of vegetable, bean, and grain side dishes. Among the types used in this book are:

Cardamom Sweet, exotic-tasting spice whose small, round seeds come enclosed inside a husklike pod. Cardamom is best purchased whole and the seeds ground with a spice grinder or in a mortar with a pestle as needed.

Cayenne Pepper Very hot ground spice derived from the dried cayenne chile.

Cinnamon Popular sweet spice derived from the aromatic bark of a type of evergreen tree. It is sold ground or as whole dried strips called cinnamon sticks.

Cloves Rich and aromatic East African spice used whole or in its ground form to flavor sweet and savory recipes.

Coriander Small, spicy-sweet seeds of the coriander plant, used whole or ground.

Cumin Spice with a strong, dusky, aromatic flavor sold ground or as small, crescent-shaped seeds. The seeds can be ground with a spice grinder or a mortar and pestle as needed.

Nutmeg Hard pit of the fruit of the nutmeg tree, commonly purchased already ground. Whole nutmeg, below, can be ground as needed, using a special nutmeg grater.

Paprika Powdered spice derived from the dried paprika pepper, available in sweet, mild, and hot forms. Hungarian paprika is the best; milder Spanish paprika may also be used.

Saffron Intensely aromatic, golden orange spice made from the dried stigmas of a species of crocus. Sold either as threads—the dried stigmas—or in powdered form. For the best quality, look for products labeled "pure saffron."

Index

❦

ACKNOWLEDGMENTS

The following authors provided the recipes for this book: Joyce Goldstein: pages 16, 20,
23, 29, 32, 34, 37, 40, 43, 44, 52, 57, 63, 65, 66, 75, 76, 79, 82, 91, 97, 98, 100, 103;
Chuck Williams: 39, 47, 49, 50, 55, 58, 61, 70, 73, 86, 89; Emanuela Stucchi Prinetti: pages 15, 19, 24, 27;
John Phillip Carroll: pages 31, 92, 95; Jacqueline Mallorca: 81, 85; and the Scotto Sisters: page 69.
The publishers thank the following people for their generous assistance and support in producing this book:
Desne Border, Ken DellaPenta, Julia Schlosser, Elizabeth Ruegg, Nette Scott, William Shaw, Elizabeth C. Davis,
Danielle Di Salvo, Kim Konecny, Laura Ferguson, Sue White, and Andrea Lucich.
The following kindly lent props for the photography: Williams-Sonoma, Pottery Barn,
Chuck Williams, Sue Fisher King, Biordi Art Imports, and Fillamento.
The publishers also thank all the other individuals and organizations that provided
props, locations, and other assistance in producing this book.

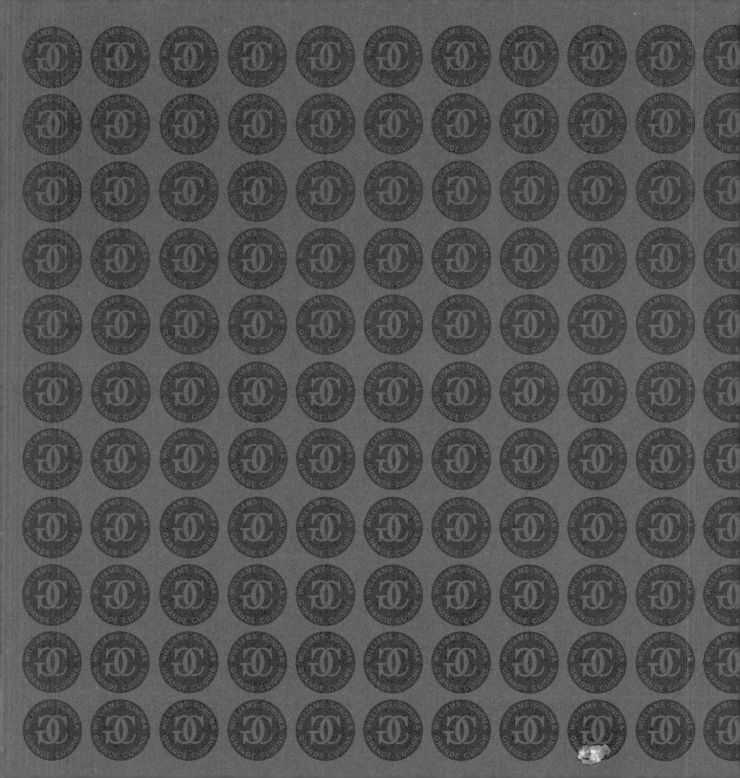